T0063558

Richan's Miracle

Janet Robinson

BALBOA.
PRESS

A DIVISION OF HAY HOUSE

ISBN: 978-1-4525-4911-8 (sc)
ISBN: 978-1-4525-4910-1 (e)

Library of Congress Control Number: 2012906419

Balboa Press books may be ordered through booksellers or by contacting:

Balboa Press
A Division of Hay House
1663 Liberty Drive
Bloomington, IN 47403
www.balboapress.com
1-(877) 407-4847

Because of the dynamic nature of the Internet, any web addresses or links contained in this book may have changed since publication and may no longer be valid. The views expressed in this work are solely those of the author and do not necessarily reflect the views of the publisher, and the publisher hereby disclaims any responsibility for them.

The author of this book does not dispense medical advice or prescribe the use of any technique as a form of treatment for physical, emotional, or medical problems without the advice of a physician, either directly or indirectly. The intent of the author is only to offer information of a general nature to help you in your quest for emotional and spiritual well-being. In the event you use any of the information in this book for yourself, which is your constitutional right, the author and the publisher assume no responsibility for your actions.

Any people depicted in stock imagery provided by Thinkstock are models, and such images are being used for illustrative purposes only.
Certain stock imagery © Thinkstock.

Printed in the United States of America

Balboa Press rev. date: 04/06/12

For Richan, who survived three strokes between 1999-2001. May the Lord ever enfold you with His love.

Mom

Hi! My name is Richan, R-I-C-H-A-N, and I am 5 years old. I am in the hospital because I am very sick. There is something wrong with my brain. I had a stroke and even had a few seizures.

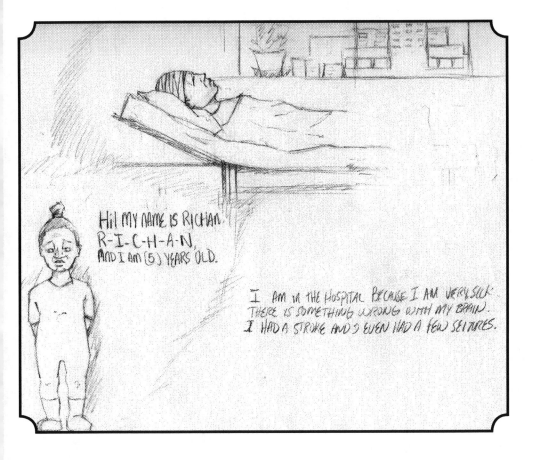

Hi! MY NAME IS RICHAN.
R-I-C-H-A-N,
AND I AM (5) YEARS OLD.

I AM IN THE HOSPITAL BECAUSE I AM VERY SICK.
THERE IS SOMETHING WRONG WITH MY BRAIN.
I HAD A STROKE AND I EVEN HAD A FEW SEIZURES.

When I couldn't move around I was very upset and I wanted to go home. I really hated being in the hospital.

However, when I started to get better I found out the most amazing thing: the hospital can be a grrreat place to be!

HOWEVER, WHEN I STARTED TO GET BETTER
I FOUND OUT THE MOST AMAZING THING.
THE HOSPITAL CAN BE A GRRREAT PLACE TO BE.

WHEN I COULDN'T MOVE AROUND
I WAS VERY UPSET AND I WANTED
TO GO HOME. I REALLY HATED
BEING IN THE HOSPITAL.

When I just got sick they used a stretcher to take me around. As I improved, I used a wheelchair.

Now that I can walk again, I sometimes like to trick my mommy and ask for a wheelchair when we go for a walk because I really enjoy the ride. Even my cousin gets to push me around sometimes.

NOW THAT I CAN WALK AGAIN, I
SOMETIMES LIKE TO TRICK MY MOMMY
AND ASK FOR A WHEELCHAIR WHEN
WE GO FOR A WALK, BECAUSE I
REALLY ENJOY THE RIDE. EVEN MY COUSIN
GETS TO PUSH ME AROUND SOMETIMES.

I love to go to the playroom on my ward. We get to paint, colour, draw, read, play, watch television and do other fun things.

I like the volunteers. They help me to do and make all kinds of fun things. They also keep me company and read me lots of stories.

Sometimes I go to the Library when it is story time. We get to listen to the neatest stories which are read by some doctors. NEAT!

Then I get to choose and sign out all my favourite books like **Arthur**, **Franklin** and so many more.

I think I drive my Mom nuts because some days I borrow five books and she has to read them all to me.

I like the volunteers. They help me to do and make all kinds of fun things. They also keep me company and read me lots of stories.

Sometimes I go to the library when it's story time. We get to listen to the neatest stories which are read by some doctors. Neat!

Then I get to choose and sign out all my favourite books — like Arthur's, Franklin, and so many more. I think I drive my mummy nuts because some days I borrow (5) books and she has to read them all to me

I get to go to two different gyms everyday. My Mom says one is for phys---- something; it's a really long word. Mom says it's spelt: P-H-Y-S-I-O-T-H-E-R-A-P-Y. The other one is for something called O-C-C-U-P-A-T-I-O-N-A-L therapy.

I HAVE TO GO TO 2 DIFFERENT GYMS EVERY DAY. MY MOM SAYS ONE IS FOR PHYS — — SOMETHING. IT'S A REALLY LONG WORD. MOM SAYS ITS SPELT: P-H-Y-S-I-O- T-H-E-R-A-P-Y THE OTHER WORD IS FOR SOMETHING CALLED OCC-U-PATIE-O-N-A-L THERAPY.

I'm not sure what these words mean but, I do know I get to play the neatest games, bounce balls, climb, run and do all kinds of fun activities. I even play Hopscotch. I really like the gyms.

I'M NOT SURE WHAT THESE WORDS MEAN BUT I DO KNOW I GET TO PLAY THE NEATEST GAMES, BOUNCE BALLS, CLIMB, RUN, AND DO ALL KINDS OF FUN ACTIVITIES. I EVEN PLAYED HOP SKOTCH. I REALLY LIKE THE GYMG.

One of my most favourite is the evening we go to the theatre and watch the funny play put on by some doctors, nurses, and volunteers. I like all the funny-looking characters and the songs. We even get a chance to win a prize. Wow!

One of my most favorite is the evening we go to the theatre and watch the funnyplay put on by some doctors, nurses and volunteers. I like all the funny-looking characters and the songs. We even get a chance to win a prize. Wow!

The best part of being in the hospital is that I get so many visitors. They all come to see how I am doing and they bring me lots of presents, treats and cards with money!

Oh, I still don't like medicines and I really hate I.V.'s, but, as I suffer.........

THE BEST PART OF BEING IN IN THE HOSPITAL IS THAT I GET SO MANY VISITORS. THEY ALL COME TO SEE HOW I AM DOING AND THEY BRING ME LOTS OF PRESENTS, TREATS AND CARDS WITH MONEY!!

OH, I STILL DON'T LIKE MEDICINES AND I REALLY HATE I.V.'S, BUT AS I SUFFER....

...through those: I know that I'll be able to do something fun when they are done.

I can't believe it! The doctor just told my Mom that they are sending me home, TODAY!

Maybe I should pretend to get sick again!

Author's Postscript

It was the summer of 1999 when our daughter, Richan, had her first stroke. For me, at the time, it was inconceivable that a five year old could be paralyzed on one side, unable to speak, in a coma, ... We spent four weeks in hospital and months in rehab. She learned to walk, talk and to function independently again.

Then, in the spring of 2001 she had her second stroke. We went through it all again, and she recovered. What do you know? By the end of summer 2001, she had stroke number 3. Our family was devastated, but many people prayed, and miraculously, she recovered from the third stroke and is doing very well today.

I thank God for healing her. I thank all those who prayed for her. I thank all the medical personnel — hospital and rehab — who helped through her illnesses.

Janet Robinson, March 2012.

The author, Janet Robinson, is a certified Ontario teacher who enjoys writing in her spare time. She is married and lives with her family in Oshawa, Ontario.

http://www.richansmiracle.com

Mark Graham, the illustrator, lives and works in Whitby, Ontario. He works in all types of media.

Pictures

Richan just before she became ill

She's about 7 here

She's 6 years old and at a wedding with
her sisters, Shelly-Ann and Grace

She's graduating Grade
8 - June 2008

She's graduating High School - March 2012

Family picture at her Gr. 8 Grad June 2008

Additional family at Gr. 8 Grad, June 2008

Mark drew this family portrait from photographs in November of 2002

Printed in the United States
By Bookmasters